Comforting Little Hearts
Understanding Chronic Illness

When Will I Feel Better?

Written by Robin Prince Monroe
Illustrated by Trudy Calvert

CPH®
SAINT LOUIS

Comforting Little Hearts
Series Titles

Why Don't We Live Together Anymore? (Understanding Divorce)
When Will I Feel Better? (Understanding Chronic Illness)
I Have a New Family Now (Understanding Blended Families)
Balloons for Trevor (Understanding Death)

Published by Concordia Publishing House
3558 S. Jefferson Avenue, St. Louis, MO 63118-3968
Manufactured in the United States of America

1 2 3 4 5 6 7 8 9 10   07 06 05 04 03 02 01 00 99 98

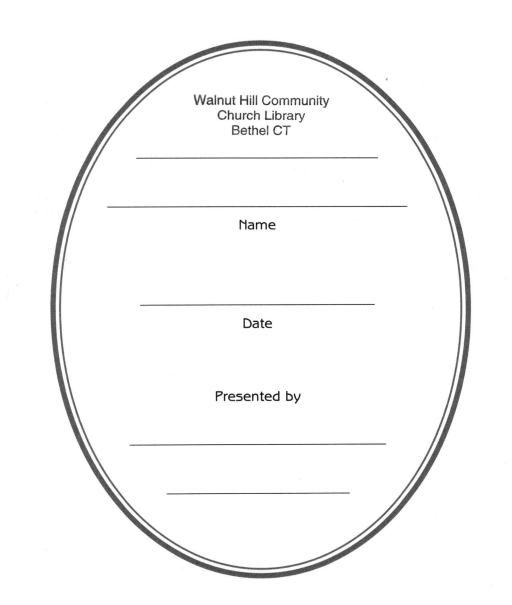

Walnut Hill Community
Church Library
Bethel CT

_____

_____

Name

_____

Date

Presented by

_____

_____

In memory of my precious daughter,
Anna Elizabeth Monroe,
whose life is still touching
the lives of others.

We all get sick sometimes.

Grandparents, parents, uncles, friends, babies, and children all get sick. Usually it doesn't take very long for us to get well.

But sometimes we are so sick that we don't get well for a long time. Or maybe we have a sickness that the doctors don't know how to fix. This is called being chronically ill.

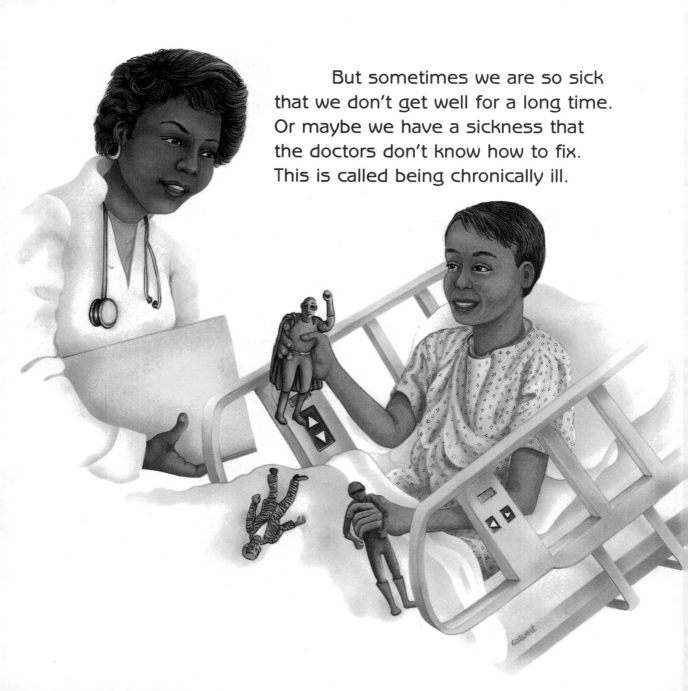

I started feeling bad on _____.

(Fill in the date.)

The doctors **know / don't know** what is wrong. (Circle one.)

I have _____, which means

_____

_____

_____

Do you know there are lots of children who are chronically ill?
Write the names of children you know who are chronically ill.

_____

_____

_____

Being sick can change the things children and their parents do each day. Maybe you will need to go to the doctor a lot or spend time in the hospital. You might have to take medicine or eat special food or do your schoolwork at home or rest more.

This is what I need to do: _____

_____

_____

_____.

When you are sick you may have many feelings. Some children feel sad. They miss feeling good and being able to go to school regularly. Sometimes they cry. It's okay to cry. Did you know Jesus cried? He did.

Some children feel angry. They get tired of being sick! They don't want to be sick anymore. It's okay to be mad. Did you know Jesus got angry? He did.

Some children feel jealous.

They see other children who don't have to take medicine
or go to the hospital. They see other children who are well,
and they want to be well too.

Some children are afraid. They are worried that they won't get better. It's okay to be afraid. Even adults get scared when they are chronically ill. God loves you no matter how you feel, and He cares about your feelings. He really does!

So do not fear, for I am with you; do not be dismayed, for I am your God. I will strengthen you and help you; I will uphold you with My righteous right hand.
Isaiah 41:10

Color the picture
that shows how you feel.

    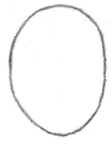

It might help you to talk to someone
about your feelings. Maybe you can talk with your
parents or your pastor, maybe a counselor, or maybe
another child or adult who is chronically ill.

I can talk to _____ about my feelings. And you can talk to God. He is *always* ready to listen.

"For I know the plans I have for you," declares the LORD, *"plans to prosper you and not to harm you, plans to give you hope and a future. Then you will call upon Me and come and pray to Me, and I will listen to you."*
Jeremiah 29:11–12

Sometimes people who are chronically ill think it is their fault. But being sick is *not* a punishment. There is sickness in the world because there is sin in the world. But Jesus died on the cross to take all the punishment for that sin. It is **NEVER** a child's fault that he or she is sick.

Say that out loud.
It is not my fault.
Louder.
It is *not* my fault!

> As [Jesus] went along, He saw a man blind from birth. His disciples asked Him, "Rabbi, who sinned, this man or his parents, that he was born blind?" "Neither this man nor his parents sinned," said Jesus, "but this happened so that the work of God might be displayed in his life."
> John 9:1–3

Sometimes when you are sick, you might feel like it doesn't matter what you do. But God has special things for all of us to do, whether we are sick or well.

These are some things you can do:

1. Write letters to grandparents, friends, missionaries, or other sick children.
2. Call people who don't get out much.
3. Paint or draw.
4. Read books.
5. Write stories or poems.
6. Work on the computer.
7. Make presents.
8. Pray.
9. Some other things I can do are

_____

_____

_____

My grace is sufficient for you,
for My power is made perfect in weakness.
2 Corinthians 12:9

Some of God's helpers in Bible times had chronic illnesses. They knew God loved them and would help them to share His love. Read about one of them—Paul—in your Bible or Bible storybook. He told people all over the world about God's love.

He will wipe every tear from their eyes.
There will be no more death or mourning or
crying or pain, for the old order of things
has passed away.
Revelation 21:4

Sometimes being sick makes us hurt. That can be the hardest thing about illness. Many times other people don't know what the pain feels like. But Jesus knows everything about your pain. He is there feeling it with you, and He promises that you will not hurt this way forever.

God gives you good things every day—
even when you are sick.

Like little flowers hiding in the
weeds, you might have to look hard
to find them, but they are there. Their
bright petals peek through the thorns.

One good thing about today is _____

_____

_____

_____

Finally, brothers, whatever is true, whatever is noble, whatever is right, whatever is pure, whatever is lovely, whatever is admirable— if anything is excellent or praiseworthy—think about such things.

Philippians 4:8

Keep a little notebook by your bed.
Each day write a sentence or draw a picture
about one good thing God does for you.

It *is* hard being sick. Sometimes it feels like
you are carrying a very heavy weight around all day long.
But you don't have to carry it by yourself. Jesus will carry
your sickness for you.

Jesus will watch over you while you are sleeping. He will go with you to the doctor. He will go with you to the hospital. He will be with you while you are getting x-rays and tests. He will go with you into the operating room. And He will go with you when you get to go home.

If I go up to the heavens, You are there;
if I make my bed in the depths, You are there.
If I rise on the wings of the dawn, if I settle on
the far side of the sea, even there Your hand
will guide me, Your right hand will hold me fast.
Psalm 139:8–10

Jesus will make you strong and He will never leave you alone.

*Even youths grow tired and weary,
and young men stumble and fall; but those
who hope in the Lord will renew their strength.
They will soar on wings like eagles; they will run
and not grow weary, they will walk and not be faint.*
Isaiah 40:30–31

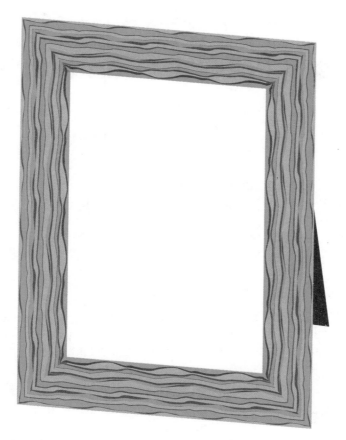

Draw a picture of yourself well.

What would you like to do when you are well?

Write some things here: _____

_____.

How Parents Can Help

by Gena Haskell,
a certified child life specialist
who deals with chronic illness herself

Pray. Ask God to give you strength to endure the path ahead of you. Ask family and friends to pray. Encourage your child to go to Jesus with her feelings. Search God's Word for His promises and share them with your child.

Allow yourself and your child to cry. Tears are cleansing and can actually help you see things more clearly. Crying is appropriate and a part of the healing process.

Journal your thoughts and feelings. Writing can be quite therapeutic. Express your emotions on paper, journaling the good as well as the hard times. Encourage your child to journal too. If he is too young to write, help him express his feelings through drawing or painting. Art can help a child release many pent-up feelings.

Take one day at a time. Set short-term goals that are realistic and attainable. Try to be flexible, and avoid being overprotective. Let your child's activities be as normal as possible. Let her attend school as often as she can and encourage playtime with peers.

Be honest. Your child must know he can trust you in this uncertain and unfamiliar phase of his life. Tell your child the name of the illness. It is easier to fight when you know what you are fighting. Verbalize the facts and dispel any myths about the illness.

Maintain structure. Although some guidelines must be altered, try to maintain the same family rules and discipline that were in place prior to the diagnosis. Children feel a sense of security when guidelines are maintained.

Make time for your spouse and well children. Family members often feel overlooked during an illness. Avoid letting siblings be the last to know the diagnosis or test results. Nurture your marriage. Children gain strength and security from witnessing your love for each other.

Make memories. Don't wait for the "perfect" time to plan family activities. Be creative. Think of new ways to have fun together.

Involve your child in the decision-making process. As much as possible, let your child have a say in decisions that pertain to her medical needs. If medications or therapy must be administered at home, let your child help decide where the treatments will occur. Keep one room, if possible her bedroom or playroom, off-limits to procedures. She needs one place to call her own, a haven from medical demands. It is especially good if her bed can remain a safe place to be.

Embrace humor. Laughter can have a remarkable, healing effect on your heart and mind. Watch funny movies, read humorous books, and surround yourself and your child with friends that make you laugh.